LEONARDO DA VINCI

LADY WITH AN ERMINE

CIRCA 1492.
ART IN THE AGE OF EXPLORATION

NATIONAL GALLERY OF ART, WASHINGTON
OCTOBER 1991—JANUARY 1992

LEONARDO DA VINCI

(1452-1519)

LADY WITH AN ERMINE

FROM THE CZARTORYSKI COLLECTION
NATIONAL MUSEUM, CRACOW

CATALOGUE EDITED

BY

JÓZEF GRABSKI
JANUSZ WAŁEK

VIENNA—**IRSA**—CRACOW
1991

PUBLISHED BY:

IRSA Verlag GmbH, Rüdengasse 6, A–1030 Vienna, Austria
Tel.: (0 222) 7 130 136; Fax (0 222) 7 130 130

TRANSLATION AND EDITING:

Witold CZARTORYSKI
Mary FILIPPI
Cara M. MORRIS
Krystyna STANKIEWICZ

PHOTOGRAPHS:

Marek GARDULSKI, ZPAF, Cracow
Łukasz SCHUSTER, Cracow

CATALOGUE LAYOUT:

Maria Bogna GRABSKA
Karol GRABSKI

Copyright © by IRSA 1991. Printed in Austria by Rauchdruck , Innsbruck

ISBN 3–900731–42–X

PREFACE

This catalogue was prepared as an accompaniment for Leonardo da Vinci's *Portrait of a Lady with an Ermine* on the longest journey in its 500-year history—from the historical Polish city of Cracow to the National Gallery of Art in Washington, where it is currently on loan as one of the highlights of the exhibition "Circa 1492. Art in the Age of Exploration" (October 1991—January 1992).

IRSA Publishing House is extremely grateful to all those involved in the creation of the catalogue, especially Janusz Wałek, Curator of Painting at the National Museum in Cracow, and Director of the Czartoryski Collection, who planned the general concept and oversaw the editorial work. The texts he has chosen reflect the body of modern Polish research into the painting, including analysis of thorough scientific examinations, and in most cases the essays, though previously published elsewhere, will here be accessible for the first time to an international readership. Janusz Wałek has of necessity edited and abridged them to avoid repetitions.

IRSA sincerely thanks the former longtime Director of the Czartoryski Collection and present Polish Minister of Culture, Marek Rostworowski, for his support and goodwill during the catalogue's preparation, as well as David Alan Brown, Curator of Italian Renaissance Painting at the National Gallery of Art in Washington.

Thanks are also due Dorota Dec and Anna Krawczyk of the Czartoryski Museum in Cracow, Barbara Szyper for her editing of the technical texts, and Andrzej Starmach of the Starmach Gallery in Cracow.

IRSA would like to acknowledge with particular gratitude the translating and editorial work of Dr. Witold Czartoryski, without whose help this catalogue would not have been possible.

JÓZEF GRABSKI
Director, IRSA

Vienna, September 1991

INTRODUCTION

The Cracow painting by Leonardo da Vinci, best known as the *Lady with an Ermine*, has intrigued viewers for 500 years. It is generally accepted as a portrait of the beautiful and intelligent Cecilia Gallerani, mistress of Ludovico Sforza, Duke of Milan. One of his nicknames was "il Ermellino" (the ermine).

Cecilia sat for her portrait by Leonardo when she was still a very young girl—"in una età si imperfecta," as she wrote in a letter to Isabella d'Este. The hunting ferret held in her arms was later referred to as an ermine. This would imply the encoded presence in the picture not only of the ducal lover but also of Cecilia herself, for the Greek word for ermine, *galē*, forms the first two syllables of her family name Gallerani. In order to represent the wild ermine the artist might have used a tame ferret as a model. A ferret is slightly larger than an ermine but is otherwise similar. *Se non e vero, e ben trovato.*

The romantic, intellectually gifted Princess Isabella Czartoryska liked to think of the painting in her possession as representing "la belle ferronnière," an ironmonger's daughter who had been a favorite of King François I of France, and whose supposed portrait, attributed to Leonardo, is in the Louvre. The *Lady with an Ermine* was presented to Isabella by her son Prince Adam Jerzy Czartoryski, who was a friend and adviser to the future Tsar Alexander I. As Russian ambassador to the Kingdom of Sardinia, Czartoryski travelled around Italy where he bought two portraits, that of Cecilia painted by Leonardo, and that of a young man by Raphael. Isabella was in the process of founding a museum at her palace at Puławy, and it was there that both paintings were deposited.

Three decades later, the same Prince Czartoryski presided over the Polish government in an armed uprising against Russia. During one of the first battles the *Lady with an Ermine* was evacuated from Puławy to save it from Russian bombardment. For fear of its confiscation by the tsar, the painting was walled up in a niche of another family residence, Sieniawa Palace on the river San. Later taken to Paris via Dresden, the painting found refuge in the Hôtel Lambert, where the exiled prince lived on the Île Saint-Louis. The picture finally emerged from obscurity when it was moved to the Czartoryski Museum, which had been reestablished, this time in Cracow, by Adam Jerzy's son Władysław in 1876.

In 1914, in the face of a possible Russian occupation of Cracow and the renewed threat of confiscation, the painting was sent to the Royal Gallery in Dresden for safekeeping during the First World War. It was reclaimed in 1920, not without resistance on the part of the German authorities.

In August 1939, on the eve of the Second World War, it was evacuated from Cracow again, and to the same Sieniawa Palace where it had been concealed a little over a century before. German soldiers soon broke into the hiding place, but they were mainly interested in the gold they found there and left the picture behind. The abandoned painting was rescued from the demolished cellar by a serving maid of the great-great-grandson of Princess Isabella, Augustyn Czartoryski, and his wife, Dolores de Borbon.

To keep it out of the hands of the Soviets, what remained of the Czartoryski collections after the looting was quickly removed to the western bank of the river San, but it again fell prey to the Germans. The *Lady with an Ermine* was sent to Berlin, and from there to Cracow, where it ended up at the Wawel Royal Castle, now serving as the residence of the Nazi governor Hans Frank, who received the picture as a gift from Hitler. When Frank fled Cracow in January 1945 he took the portrait with him to his villa at Schliersee in Bavaria, where he was arrested by the Americans. The painting was taken into storage in Munich, joining works of art looted by the Germans from all over Europe. By 1946 the portrait was back in Cracow, only to be transferred in 1952 to the National Museum in Warsaw as part of a government plan to centralize the country's art holdings. A couple of years later, however, an air-conditioned railway carriage brought the *Lady with an Ermine* home to Cracow in triumph.

Today, following an agreement on the part of the collection's heir, Prince Adam Carlos Czartoryski, the great-great-great-grandson of Isabella, and a promise made to U.S. President George Bush by Polish President Lech Wałęsa during his visit to Washington, the beautiful lady is embarking on an air journey over the ocean crossed by Christopher Columbus five centuries ago. Her destination is the exhibition "Circa 1492. Art in the Age of Exploration" at the National Gallery of Art in Washington, commemorating the discovery of America.

Numerous previous requests to exhibit the painting abroad were always turned down, with the exception of a trip the portrait made to Moscow. This time, in view of the special nature of the anniversary and the enormous authority of the participants to the agreement, the Czartoryski Museum has given its approval for the loan.

Next year, in return, the National Gallery will lend the Czartoryski Museum the *Portrait of Bindo Altoviti* by Raphael on the occasion of the Month of European Culture in Cracow. That portrait is similar to Raphael's *Portrait of a Young Man* which Prince Adam Jerzy Czartoryski brought back from Italy together with the painting by Leonardo. Isabella Czartoryska, aware of the closeness between the two Raphaels, included an engraving of Altoviti's portrait in the catalogue of her Museum. Sadly, the Museum's own Raphael was stolen by the Nazis and subsequently lost. How thankful we are that a happier fate awaited the *Lady with an Ermine*.

MAREK ROSTWOROWSKI
Minister of Culture and Art
of the Republic of Poland

Warsaw, September 11, 1991

1) Leonardo da Vinci, *Lady with an Ermine*, oil on walnut panel, 534 x 393 mm., Czartoryski Collection, Cracow.

SELECTED SOURCES

A sonnet by Bernardo Bellincioni (? – 1492):

Di che t'adiri a chi invidia hai Natura!
Al Vinci che ha ritratto una tua stella!
Cecilia se belissima oggi è quella
Che a suoi begli occhi il sole par ombra oscura.

L'onor è tuo, sebben con sua pittura
La fa che par che ascolti, e non favella.
Pensa, quanto sarà più viva e bella,
Più a te sia gloria nell' età futura.

Ringraziar dunque Lodovico or puoi
L'ingegno e la man di Lionardo,
Che a posteri di lei voglion far parte.

Chi lei vedra cosi benchè sia tardo
Vederla viva, dira: Basta a noi
Comprender or quel ch'è natura ed arte.

Why are you angry, Nature, whom do you envy?
Vinci, he who has portrayed one of your stars!
Cecilia is today the one most beautiful
Whose splendid eyes cast the sun into shadow.

The honor is yours, though in his painting
She seems to listen but she does not speak.
Think of it, the more alive and beautiful she is,
The greater will be your glory in the future.

So be grateful, Lodovico,
For the genius and skill of Leonardo
Which desire to give a part of her to posterity.

He who sees her, even if it is too late
To see her alive, will say: this is enough for us
To understand what Nature and art are about.

An exchange of letters between Isabella d'Este and Cecilia Gallerani:

Isabella d'Este to Cecilia Gallerani (April 26, 1498):

> *Having seen today some fine portraits by the hand of Giovanni Bellini, we began to discuss the works of Leonardo, and wished we could compare them with these paintings. And since we remember that he painted your likeness, we beg you to be so good as to send us your portrait by this messenger whom we have dispatched on horseback, so that we may not only be able to compare the works of the two masters but also have the pleasure of seeing your face again. The picture will be returned to you afterwards, with our most grateful thanks for your kindness....*

2) Leonardo da Vinci, *Portrait of Isabella d'Este*, 1500, detail, Louvre, Paris.

Cecilia Gallerani to Isabella d'Este (April 29, 1498):

> *I have read Your Highness's letter, and since you wish to see my portrait, I send it without delay and would send it with even greater pleasure if it were more like me. But Your Highness must not think this proceeds from any defect in the master, for indeed I think there is no other painter to equal him in the world, but merely because the portrait was painted when I was much younger. Since then I have greatly changed, so that if you saw the picture and myself together, you would never believe it could be meant for me. All the same, Your Highness will, I hope, accept this proof of my goodwill and believe that I am ready and anxious to gratify your wishes....*

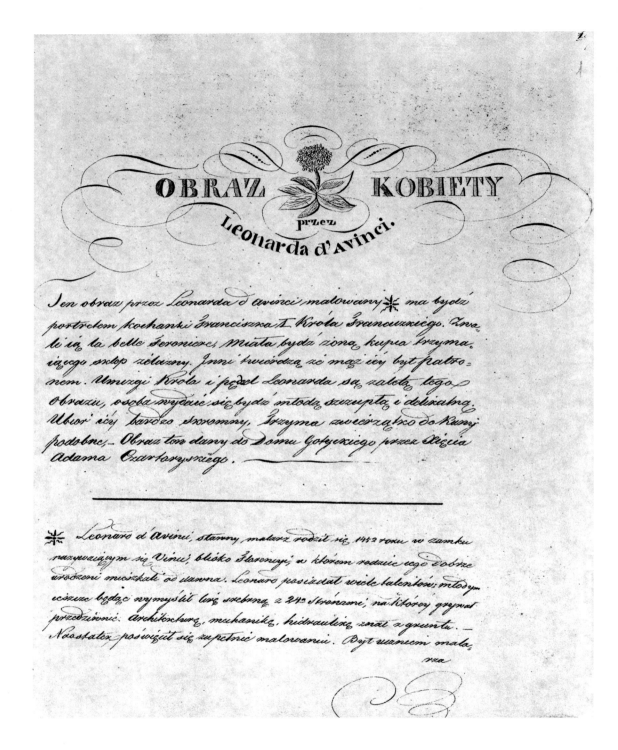

4) Catalogue entries in the hand of Princess Isabella Czartoryska for her museum at Puławy.

From the catalogue for the Czartoryski Museum in Puławy, written *c.* 1809 by Princess Isabella Czartoryska:

> *The picture painted by Leonardo d'Avinci is supposed to be the portrait of the mistress of François I, King of France. She was called La Belle Ferronnière, and was believed to be the wife of an ironmonger. Others state that her husband was the patron. The attentions of the king and the brush of Leonardo give the painting its quality. The person seems to be young, slim, and delicate. Her clothes are very modest. She is holding a small animal similar to a marten. The picture was given to the "Gothic House" by Prince Adam Czartoryski.*

From the French version of the catalogue for the Czartoryski Museum:

> *This charming picture, which seems to be a portrait, was painted by the famous Leonardo da Vinci. It was given to me by my oldest son, who brought it from Italy. It represents a girl holding a small animal to her breast. The extraordinary truthfulness of the whole figure, her natural and relaxed posture, a coloring which can be seen only in the works of this great painter, make this painting—which in spite of its age is preserved in perfect condition—extremely valuable. The small animal held by the young girl is difficult to describe. If it were a dog it would be ugly, if it is another type of animal it is unknown to me. It is white and has quite small paws and a relatively large head. The young girl appears to be about fifteen years old, of delicate frame, and seemingly in fragile health. A simple band holds her hair and the whole effect is of a portrait painted from nature rather than the imagination.*

Isabella Czartoryska authored the following summary of Leonardo da Vinci's life for her catalogue. Composed in a sentimental style, it is probably the first biographical account of the artist to appear in Poland.

> *Leonardo da Vinci, the famous painter, was born in 1452 at the castle called Vinci, near Florence, where his well-born parents had lived for a long time. Leonardo was possessed of many talents. While still young he invented the silver lyre with 24 strings, which he played in a very strange way. He had a thorough knowledge of architecture, mechanics, and hydraulics. Eventually he devoted himself wholly to painting. He was the pupil of the painter called Verrocchio. His work* The Last Supper *which he painted in the Dominican refectory in Milan, combines all the beauties and it remains a masterpiece of painting. Being angry at the prior because he pushed him to work more quickly, [Leonardo] took revenge on him by giving his face to Judas. Together with Michelangelo he painted the Senate chamber in Florence.*
>
> *Finally disappointed because of the envy of some of his fellow painters, he left Italy and moved to France where François I received him with pleasure and kept him there by his side. He died in Fontainebleau in 1519 in the arms of the king, who honored and loved him. He had a beautiful and splendid figure, he had supernatural powers, and was of sweet manner and full of knowledge. When the French noblemen showed their astonishment that François I held him in his arms in his final agony, the king said to them: "It is not very difficult to have people like you, but a man like Leonardo da Vinci is very rarely given to us by Providence."*

JANUSZ WAŁEK

Leonardo the Explorer

Leonardo da Vinci (1452–1519) belonged to an age of discovery. Navigators were sailing the oceans, while at home philosophers broke with medieval tradition to look at the mysteries of the human spirit from a new, "scientific" perspective. In Italy, the great pioneers of the modern world included Marco Polo, St. Francis of Assisi, Dante, and Giotto, but artists in the Netherlands also paved the way for the explosion of intellectual curiosity and creative experimentation that was the Renaissance.

It was in Florence that a revolutionary vision of man and his place in the world emerged in the work of Brunelleschi, Masaccio, Donatello, Alberti, and others in the first half of the fifteenth century. Year after year the horizons—mental, artistic, geographic—were extended to accommodate ever more ambitious discoveries. Yet at the same time as this feverish expansion of knowledge was under way, numerous Italian duchies and cities were in a state of permanent war—and rulers were often just as interested in the development of more efficient weaponry as they were in promoting the arts.

Two landmark events are usually seen as opening up the modern era: Gutenberg's invention of movable type printing, and Christopher Columbus's 1492 voyage to what was for the Europeans a New World.

Information was no longer the exclusive possession of a privileged few. For the first time books could be reproduced in large quantities and widely distributed. And the existence of a previously unknown continent forced Europeans to radically redefine the boundaries of what they thought they knew.

There remained still another secret to unlock but it too was revealed by the first half of the next century, when the Polish astronomer Nicolaus Copernicus proved that the Earth orbits the sun and not the other way round. This readjustment of the world's place in the universe was one more jolt to man's sense of his place in the world.

And where does Leonardo da Vinci fit into all this? Was he only an artist, fulfilling commissions from powerful princes for handsome remuneration, just as his contemporaries did? Or was he an empirical researcher into the laws of nature who used art as a methodological tool?

In offering his services to Ludovico Sforza, Duke of Milan, Leonardo wrote that he knew how to construct a war machine and build walls that would protect a city

5) Leonardo da Vinci, *Virgin and Child with St. Anne*, 1501–03, detail, Louvre, Paris.

6) Leonardo da Vinci, *Virgin of the Rocks*, 1483–86, detail, Louvre, Paris.

from attack. Almost as an afterthought, he added that, in times of peace, he could turn his hand to artistic activity as well.

Leonardo left relatively few paintings and nowadays only about ten works are attributed with any certainty to him. However, he filled innumerable notebook pages with his secret mirror writing, and we have thousands of drawings and charts on everything from the complex structure of rocks and the properties of air, water, and clouds, to the development of a human embryo.

Can all these studies be treated as works of art? The answer is emphatically yes, thanks to the subtlety and refinement of his line, the charm of his shapes, of his lights and shadows; but we must keep in mind that the sketches are basically notes made to support the memory and feed the imagination of a scientist. They are the fruit of Leonardo's lifelong commitment to the investigation of nature.

Similarly, the paintings can also be seen as notes of a kind. They may illustrate problems of perspective, as in the unfinished *Adoration of the Magi* (Uffizi Gallery, Florence); feature technical experiments, as in *The Last Supper* (refectory of Santa Maria delle Grazie, Milan); or demonstrate how to depict the bodies of a man and a horse in motion, as in *The Battle of Anghiari* (Palazzo Vecchio, Florence), a wall painting now lost and best known from a copy by Peter Paul Rubens (Louvre, Paris).

Above all, Leonardo strove to paint the human face as a mirror of the soul [Figs. 5, 6]. When painting *The Last*

7) Leonardo da Vinci, *The Annunciation*, 1479–81, detail, Uffizi Gallery, Florence.

8) Leonardo da Vinci, *Ginevra de' Benci*, 1474–76, detail, National Gallery of Art, Washington.

Supper, for example, he went to great lengths to find a sitter for Judas whose face could adequately convey the inner evil of the Apostle who betrayed Jesus. Mary appears in *The Annunciation* (Uffizi Gallery, Florence) [Fig. 7] as an innocent young girl quite startled by the appearance of the angel. Roused from the life she has lived up till now as if in a dream, she reacts apprehensively—in contrast to the angel, who is perfectly calm in his full knowledge of the mystery. In the *Portrait of Ginevra de' Benci* (National Gallery of Art, Washington) [Fig. 8], the sitter looks to be a girl of uncomplicated character, standing on the threshold of womanhood. The subject of the *Portrait of a Lady with an Ermine* may be someone with rather more experience, as attested by the sharp, alert look in her eyes. She is probably

a member of a court. Whoever was the model for the *Mona Lisa* (Louvre, Paris), she and her smile suggest an inner harmony, possibly achieved in the course of a quiet, passionless life.

Was Leonardo simply an artist or a systematic observer of the world who used the results of his research in his art? Did he create art for art's own sake, or did he regard it as only one of the instruments with which to understand the world?

Leonardo's famous drawing of *Homo quadratus* (Accademia, Venice) [Fig. 9] shows a naked, long-haired man—probably Leonardo himself—inserted into two geometric figures, a circle and a square. The man spreads his arms and legs to touch the borders of the world that can be measured by science. He is somewhat reminiscent of the crucified Christ—or a navigator giving signals from a ship. The man is sealed within the circle and square. Isolated by his knowledge and his art, Leonardo was lonely all his life. "Quando sarai solo—sarai tutto tuo," he wrote (When you are alone you will belong wholly to yourself).

In the *Lady with an Ermine*, two very important problems are successfully resolved: first, how to overcome the material, artificial nature of a picture—here, merely a bit of wood covered with paint; and second, how to capture a fleeting moment from life and fix it in a work of art forever.

The brilliant manner in which Leonardo met the first challenge evokes Leon Battista Alberti's famous definition of a picture—that it is nothing but a hole in the wall through which we look at nature. Here the real world is recreated in all its three-dimensionality on the flat walnut panel. Behind the surface, there is the illusion of life. Everything represented is true to its nature. The skin of the sitter is smooth, but underneath we can sense the bone structure, the tension of the muscles, and the course of the veins, all testifying to the artist's grasp of anatomy. Real also are the softness of the animal's fur, the sharpness of its claws, the young lady's glistening eyes, the different textures of her garments, the sleeves festooned with ribbons, the taut fillet, and the sheer, almost invisible veil covering the upper part of her forehead.

It is not clear whether the source of light is a window or, as I would propose, a lamp or candle. This light falls from the right, illuminating the parts of the sitter's body that are turned towards it: her face, her left arm, her right hand stroking the animal and therefore slightly raised from the plane of her torso. The parts of her body that are turned away from the light, such as her right elbow and her partially hidden left hand, as well as the rear part of the animal's body, are in semi-darkness and accordingly lose their shape. The colors in the strongly lit areas are vibrant, while in the weakly lit areas they nearly disappear. This objective law of the interdependence of light, color, and form, which was already noted by Alberti in his *Treatise on Painting*, is here rigorously applied, perhaps for the first time in painting. Leonardo thus would have achieved one of the most important discoveries in art.

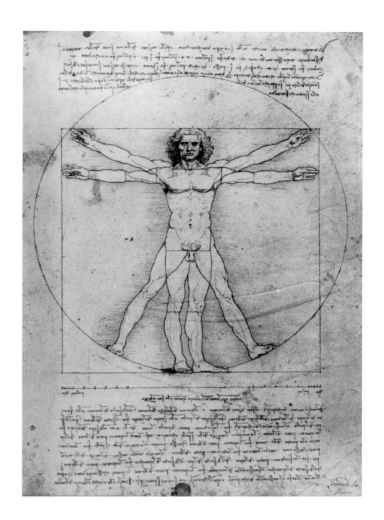

9) Leonardo da Vinci, *Homo quadratus*, 1492, Accademia, Venice.

If the artist's intention was indeed to make a conscious study of the effects of artificial light, then the *Lady with an Ermine* represents a breakthrough in this area. Geertgen tot sint Jans and Piero della Francesca had experimented with dramatic indoor lighting effects but only later would true solutions evolve in the works of Caravaggio and Georges de la Tour.

Although Leonardo's painting was retouched probably in the eighteenth century, technical examinations have shown that there never was a landscape as had sometimes been supposed. Rather, the original background was painted dark blue, implying an interior setting. So the portrait can be seen as a study of the effects of specific physical conditions, and the selection of these conditions as a creative decision to seek the best possible solutions for the composition of the painting and thereby heighten its artistic value.

The second problem mentioned above as having been solved in this work concerns the preservation of a transient moment of life in art. A lady playing with an animal was once observed performing that gesture of delicately pressing it to her bosom to prevent its running away. She was caught holding a steady gaze, in a state of attentiveness (perhaps she is listening to someone or something?). The artist saw her features lit in a certain way. And these impressions were for him indelible.

So does the portrait do no more than tell us that the subject was fond of animals and faithfully record her style of dress? When we stand before this picture, either in Cracow or in Washington, we don't need to be absolutely sure of the identity of the sitter—it doesn't matter whether she is or isn't Cecilia Gallerani. The picture puts us in touch with a vanished moment in time which, by virtue of having been saved by the observer and transformed into art, becomes eternal.

From this perspective, Leonardo is the discoverer of the same beautiful truth later proclaimed by Marcel Proust—that the swift passage of time in a human life can be arrested in art alone.

Leonardo aimed at a recreation of the world in the *Lady with an Ermine*. Even at close range the brushstrokes are all but invisible, except perhaps in parts of the animal's fur. The superb technical skill involved is deliberately concealed; traces of the brush and the artist's fingerprints—for he modelled the freshly laid paint with his fingers—can be seen only under magnification.

The picture was in many ways far ahead of its time. No one but Leonardo painted like that in the late fifteenth century, and no one else could have. This is perhaps the strongest argument for Leonardo's authorship of the work. It is a curiously modern portrait, with psychological interest and a dramatic impact that is heightened by the sitter's position as well as the lighting. Thus, the presence of the *Lady with an Ermine* at an exhibition on discoveries is surely not accidental.

MAREK ROSTWOROWSKI

Leonardo da Vinci's *Lady with an Ermine*

The *Portrait of the Lady with an Ermine* in the Czartoryski Collection in Cracow has been the subject of widely divergent opinions. Some have rated it a masterpiece, while others have judged it as an almost second-rate work suffering from a number of flaws. But interest has focused mainly on the question of its authorship, resulting in the search for arguments for or against an attribution to Leonardo da Vinci, whose name is inscribed in the upper left corner of the picture. For many foreign scholars with easy access to the world's leading museum collections, the Cracow portrait's unverified authorship by Leonardo has been the main hold on their attention. In Poland, however, although the question of authorship is also under discussion, the artistic value of the work itself has attracted relatively more interest, as it is the most perfect Renaissance painting in Polish hands today.

The portrait is painted in oil on a thin walnut panel measuring 534 x 393 mm. It is a three-quarter representation of a young woman, with her torso turned to the left and the head turned to the right. She holds an ermine on her left arm, and gently touches the back of its neck with her right hand. She wears a square-cut red gown with black braiding on the edges and laced with black ribbons on the arms.

The wrinkled sleeves of the white blouse are visible through the slits on the elbows. From the left arm hangs a blue cape lined in gold. The neck is adorned with a double string of black beads, one of which hangs down to her breast.

The hair, combed smooth, pinned up in the back of the neck, and tied under the chin, is held by a net and bound with a black velvet fillet. The background is evenly black. In the upper left corner can be seen the inscription "La Bele Feroniere. Leonard d'Awinci" in grey paint. In the lower left corner is a signature consisting of initials in dark grey paint.

The painting's condition is generally good, although certain parts are repainted and traces of restorations are noticeable. The repainted and distorted places include: the black background, the outline of the girl's left hand and abdomen, the paws and head of the ermine, the black shadows on the blue cape, the dark grey paint of the ribbons at the slits, the strands of hair bound under the chin, the filling in of the cracks, the washed and stippled parts

10) Leonardo da Vinci, *Lady with an Ermine*, detail.

the darkness in line with the turn to the right, gaining in plasticity. Her face is presented in full illumination, which glides down over her breast and hand, gradually disappearing on the lower part of her body. At the same time the illumination of the shapes enlivens the colors, their vividness and contrast effects diminishing in the shadowy parts of the painting.

The consistent distribution of light and shadow enables the tracing of the quality and the location of the light source. The window must have been relatively small, as the figure is subtly modelled by stressing a few illuminated parts. The window was placed on an axis with her gaze, or perhaps a little to the left of it, slightly above her head, because the convexities are shaded from below and underlined by the cast shadows. Together, the realistic study of light and the varied precision of the treatment of nearer and more distant details produce the illusion of space. Despite the apparent lack of depth in the painting, the distances are graded almost perceptibly.

Unfortunately, beyond the outline of the figure the panel is covered with black paint like varnish on a piece of furniture. That paint partly covers the outlines of the face and the left arm. Whoever did it had just enough sensitivity to feel the inconsistency between the background of his own creation and the original appearance of the figure. As a result, he darkened further the deepest shadows, the outlines of the shapes, and some of the details, for example the ribbons by the slits of the sleeve. Nevertheless, we can try to visualize the portrait before the repainting, when it featured a figure placed in an interior, with the background set well behind it (perhaps in greenish-browns similar to the general tones of the shadows). But we should be able to recognize its value even in its present state.

The study of shapes is conducted with a precision and objectivity typical of the works of Italian artists of the Quattrocento, although the painting differs from them fundamentally. On the basis of systematic observation, artists had learned much about the surrounding world, but they had not yet freed themselves from the medieval two-dimensional approach to painting. They composed their pictures on one plane, predetermining the distribution of figures and other elements according to the rules of geometric perspective, which made their compositions compatible with the field of human vision, as in the works

of the face, the eyes [Fig. 10], and the right hand. The upper left corner has been broken off and glued back on.

The painting's composition is based on the principle of the equilibrium of its elements, while the position of the sitter makes it dynamic. The slight twist of the arms and a more distinctive turn of the neck and eyes together convey a vivid impression that the girl has turned towards something that suddenly attracts her attention. The frozen gesture of the right hand indicates that she has been distracted from playing with the animal [Fig. 11]. The impression of motion is rendered not only by her posture but also by the way her body is illuminated, her figure positioned with her back to the light emerges from of Paolo Uccello, Bellini, and others. That consistency was the result of the application of an already available method, and not of the observation of the specific field of vision encompassed by a painting.

The revolution in this field took place in Italy only in the sixteenth century, when the main problem in painting was how to transpose a full and uniform visual experience onto the picture plane. Quattrocento realism meant the careful rendering of objects and their mutual spatial relations. For Cinquecento artists, reality consisted of the object perceived as a visual phenomenon, determined by its background as modified by the surrounding atmosphere and perceived by a specific viewer at a specific time. Through the accommodation of these conditions of the perception of a real object, its reproduction in painting gained a fuller and more artistic appearance. During the sixteenth century light became the element that coordinated the painter's synthesis of the outside world. Saturation with light or its skillful gradation became the dominant feature of paintings, whereas precision of modelling and local coloring became of secondary importance. With time, shapes came to be modified even in relation to the subjective conditions of perception, resulting even in the deformation of the depicted object.

The change in the formal approach to painting was accompanied by a new manner of composing the sitter in Italian portraiture. In principle, a portrait was supposed to render the appearance of the subject while meeting set requirements of representation. Fifteenth-century Italian portraits are still dominated by schematic patterns of presentation, consisting of the representation of the bust frontally or in profile, and even when the painting included the hands, which was then rather unusual, their composition would be conventional. That schematic pattern was replaced in the early sixteenth century by a much more relaxed posture, and even when it was still conventional, it would be more versatile, as is the case in the portraits by Raphael, Titian, and others. The newly adopted poses would underline not only the social standing but also the individual personality of the sitter.

The relaxed posture and lively movement of the figure in the *Lady with an Ermine* would have been unique even next to sixteenth-century Italian portraits; the originality is all the more striking in comparison with contemporary portraits of the last two decades of the fifteenth century.

11) Leonardo da Vinci, *Lady with an Ermine*, detail.

The positioning of the sitter was determined by the observation of nature and not by accepted convention. The feature of glancing up, as if in response to someone's entrance or utterance, is so strongly depicted in this painting that it transcends the normal level of achievement in portraits of its time. A similar capturing of a moment in life can only be found in the details of larger contemporary anecdotal compositions. The posture of the portrayed woman could almost be described as Baroque were it not for its complete neutrality. In Baroque, motion was imposed on the figures as an element of manneristically dynamized artistic form.

21

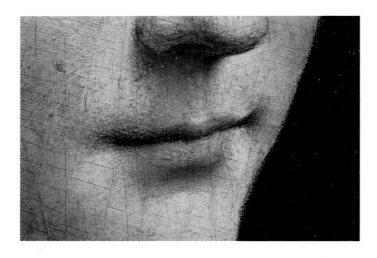

12) Leonardo da Vinci, *Lady with an Ermine*, detail.

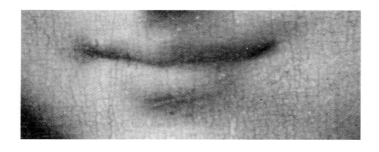

13) Leonardo da Vinci, *Mona Lisa*, 1503–05, detail, Louvre, Paris.

The revolution in painting that took place at the end of the Quattrocento is manifested by most sixteenth-century works. But the *Lady with an Ermine* seems to be one of the few pictures that actually triggered the revolution, and not just one of the many bearing the signs of its outcome. Although the artist was still attached to the concept of art typical of his time, in this painting he has achieved a synthesis of the purely visual approach to painting, fully exploiting the fifteenth-century's knowledge of nature.

The portrait shows no further traces of revolution; it is not subjectively deformed, nor does it aspire to any new style. The new style was developed somewhat later in the sixteenth century by artists who used existing knowledge to enrich the sensual and expressive side of painting, with sometimes surprising effects. But Leonardo was clearly among those who made the revolution and not someone who merely followed in its footsteps—a keen inventor and not a cool exploiter of the achievements of others.

These observations lead to the conclusion that Leonardo must have been the author of the Cracow painting, as the one artist who managed to render the complexity of sensory perception. In this way he stood up to the problems that had challenged artists throughout the fifteenth century and initiated a new orientation in art. This is documented not only by his work but by his writings as well, which are absolutely consistent with the paintings. Leonardo was more attracted to empirical knowledge than to philosophical speculation. His views on painting relied on observation and artistic practice.

Leonardo identified the beauty of colors with their intensity. He was probably the only artist of his time who consciously tried to achieve the unity of light and color. Such unity was sometimes achieved by his contemporaries, such as Giorgione with his great sensitivity to color, but none of them ever implemented it with as much determination and consistency, guided by reason, as Leonardo. He discovered that unity, examined it, put it into practice, and even developed its theoretical justification, which brought him only one step short of Cézanne's dictum "color depends on light." The signs are already apparent in the *Lady with an Ermine*.

As a result of his theory of light, Leonardo painted an image as he saw it. He warned against outlining the shapes of painted objects: "An object should not be outlined for the purpose of distinguishing it from another, it should be imposed on its own." An example of this is the head of the ermine, which is "superimposed" on flesh tones. The unknown painter who modified the original work by outlining it on its left side thereby demonstrated his lack of understanding for the innovative spirit of Leonardo's art.

The intimate association of the Cracow painting with Leonardo's conscious and almost codified artistic outlook justifies the attribution of the work to him. The close affinity of this masterpiece with fifteenth-century patterns of painting suggests a date within Leonardo's early period, such as the first years of his stay in Milan. It must have been the creation of the master himself and not that of someone in his workshop. Although Leonardo passed on his artistic theories to his pupils, especially in his "Academia Vinciana" period in Milan, none of their works can compare with the portrait's manifest depth of creative thinking.

The fundamental difference between Leonardo and his followers is that he learned from nature, whereas they learned only from him. In their pursuit of the master's excellence, they tried to accomplish the goal of comparable perfection by producing paintings resembling that ideal. But similarity to the ideal is not the same as perfection. The source of the excellence of Leonardo's works was nature, its observation and the study of its laws. The followers, instead of adopting Leonardo's method, relied rather on the available examples of his finished work and thus often lost contact with nature. Unable to grasp the essential qualities of his works, the pupils imitated the most obvious features, such as facial expressions, the lighting of a face, or hand gestures. Without analyzing the qualities of air and light, they modelled their shapes in a stiff and schematic manner. Hampered by the lack of any thorough knowledge of the human body or of the dynamics of its movements, they rendered their sitters in artificially complicated postures. Not one of them ever painted a picture that could match the Cracow painting in terms of originality and artistic value.

Although the *Lady with an Ermine* can rightly be regarded as a work by Leonardo, some inconsistencies in the painting cannot be ignored. The portrait appears to be a direct expression of Leonardo's idea of aesthetics, but some of its fragments suffer from the lack of those virtues which are the essence of Leonardo's mastery of the art. Not all parts of the portrait are equally well finished. The right sleeve and left hand, which are in shadow, were perfectly drawn but spoiled by the later addition of a broad and sketchy outline, giving the impression of Leonardo's ground.

On the other hand, the face [Fig. 10], the right hand, and the ermine [Fig. 11] were very meticulously finished indeed. The oval of the face was distorted on the right by the overlapping background, and by the added strand of hair under the chin (visible in the X-ray photograph published by Karol Estreicher). Its features are idealized in a somewhat facile manner; for example, the drawing of the eyelids is oversimplified, whereas the nose is unduly correct. The modelling of these parts combines a certain delicacy with a measure of stiffness resembling the mannerism of Ambrogio da Predis. Because of this feature some scholars have attributed the painting to him. Leonardo never resorted to any formal conventions; these tended to be used by lesser artists to compensate for less skillful observation and invention. He usually continued his work until he could solve a given artistic problem, and the work of his hand never outlasted the mental effort. The above-mentioned parts and details of the painting lack the subtlety and ingenuity of form already present in the master's earlier works, such as in the angel he painted for Verrocchio's *Baptism of Christ*; by contrast, they seem almost routine.

Although the *Lady with an Ermine* is not free of certain contradictions between some of the details and the overall character of the work, they do not suffice to undermine this writer's opinion that it is a masterpiece. The portrait's quality in terms of its artistic concept and the powerfully truthful representation of life prove that only Leonardo could have been its author.

ZDZISŁAW ŻYGULSKI, JR.

Costume Style and Leonardo's Knots in the *Lady with an Ermine*

Costume Style

To understand the costume worn by the sitter for Leonardo's *Lady with an Ermine*, it is necessary to recall the evolution of womens' fashions in Quattrocento Italy. Regional differences reflected the political disintegration of the Italian nation into several independent states, most of which were simply city-states. Nevertheless, until the middle of the fifteenth century, in some places even longer, the international court fashion originating in France and Flanders predominated in Italy: high, padded, heart- and horn-shaped headdresses or turbans; high, uncovered, and convex foreheads; small V-shaped décolletages; tight-fitting bodices; and long, trailing skirts. The style of the period can best be seen in the paintings and drawings of Antonio Pisanello, as well as in the figurative decorations on *cassoni*.

The style of the Italian Early Renaissance was established in the second half of the fifteenth century, with its chief center in Florence. It is well documented in profile portraits by Alesso Baldovinetti, Paolo Uccello, Antonio Pollaiuolo, Sandro Botticelli, and Piero della Francesca. A particularly good example is offered in the fresco portrait of Giovanna degli Albizzi by Domenico Ghirlandaio in the Florentine church of Santa Maria Novella.

In such portraits, foreheads remain uncovered, but the high Gothic headdresses have been replaced by transparent veils and nets and the hair is arranged in elaborate plaits, braids, and knots, partly flowing and richly ornamented with ribbons, fillets, and pearls and other jewelry. Blond hair prevails, being praised above all. Gowns are made of heavy, patterned brocades and velvets, with added embroidery. Bodices are still tight and laced, sleeves are tied with ribbons, decoratively slashed, and white blouses show through the slits. Skirts fall in organ-pipe pleats.

Despite the existence of their own highly developed local style, Italian women were receptive to fashions imported from abroad. Spanish influence coming via Naples, ruled by the Aragon dynasty, was especially strong.

A unique new style was born at the Castilian court around 1470. It incorporated medieval traditions, Moorish motifs, Italian Renaissance ideas, and some innovations of its own. Dark brown or black hair was generally favored, divided in two smooth waves circling the cheeks, gathered at the back in a long queue, covered on the head with a cap, the braid being hidden in a long cloth casing (called in Spanish *el tranzado*, in English pigtail). In the front the arrangement of the hair was identical with the dominant fashion for centuries among Oriental women as far as Persia and Arabia, as well as Moorish Andalusia. Braids were put into ornamented casings already in Romanesque France. The small cap at the back was fixed by a fillet across the brow.

The bodices of the Spanish gowns were similar to Italian ones but the skirts were entirely different. In 1468, when Juana de Portugal, the wife of the king of Castile, Enrique IV el Impotente, was pregnant with an illegitimate child, she invented a bell-shaped underskirt stiffened by reed hoops (*los verdugos* or *guarda-infante*, in English farthingale). A typical Spanish *los verdugos* gown was completed by a cape with one vertical opening for the arm (*sbernia*) and buskin shoes (*los chapines*), also an Oriental invention.

The fashion style *alla castellana* could only be created on Spanish soil as a successful combination of different elements in a highly organic and original form. It determined a new system of movements, poses, and gestures, contributing to the Spanish court etiquette which was soon to fascinate Europe. In a very short time the Spanish style for women had penetrated neighboring countries, appearing ephemerally in France, Flanders, England, and Germany and making its greatest conquest in Italy. It rarely kept its rigid form; more often than not, some typically Spanish features were combined with local ones. Who was capable of imitating fully the Spanish ladies?

It was about 1480 that the Spanish fashion entered Italy through Naples, and over the next ten years it reached the northern part of the country. Its path may be traced with great accuracy thanks to a profusion of literary and iconographic sources. One of the first paintings with ladies represented in Spanish style is Lorenzo Costa's *The Bentivoglio Family Before the Madonna Enthroned*, dated 1488, in the church of San Giacomo Maggiore in Bologna.

Lucrezia Borgia and Isabella and Beatrice d'Este were greatly responsible for the spread of the new fashion to northern Italy. The court of Este in Ferrara was closely connected to the Aragon court in Naples. Beatrice, daughter of Eleonore of Aragon, married the duke of Milan, Ludovico Sforza ("il Moro") in 1491, and introduced the Spanish style to Milan. Until then the ladies of Milan had worn costumes similar to the Florentine style, with some German influences (*alla tedesca*). Inspired by Beatrice, they combed their hair down in smooth waves, adopted the pigtails falling from small caps and the black fillets, and ornamented the coiffure and the neck with pearls and other jewels, favoring beads of black amber (*ambra nera*). They accepted the *sbernia*, but were not brave enough to wear the farthingales and buskin shoes.

This severely formal fashion is depicted in a great number of court portraits on panels, in miniatures, murals, marble busts, and even tiny cameos. Yet it was extinguished after Beatrice's death in 1497 and Ludovico's expulsion from Milan two years later. The most notable portraits of Milanese ladies in Spanish dress are as follows: Beatrice d'Este in the *Pala Sforzesca* (Brera Gallery, Milan) and in a bust by Gian Cristoforo Romano (Louvre, Paris); the supposed Beatrice in the *Dama alla Reticella*, school of Leonardo (Pinacoteca Ambrosiana, Milan), and in a painting by Alessandro Araldi (Uffizi Gallery, Florence); *Bona of Savoy* (The National Gallery, London); *Bianca Maria Sforza* by Ambrogio da Predis (National Gallery of Art, Washington); and Lucrezia Crivelli (?) in *La Belle Ferronnière*, school of Leonardo (Louvre) [Fig. 15].

The *Lady with an Ermine* belongs to this distinguished list. The three-quarter position of her head allows one to see only the outline of the cap and pigtail. A gauze veil held by a black fillet covers the head. The auburn hair, combed down, has lost its original wavy line and now comes under the chin due to a fault in renovation. The sitter wears a necklace of black amber. Her gown, maroon in color, is embroidered in patterns of knots and loops. The black lines in the front of the bodice and the tapes of the sleeves are unfortunately repainted. She also has a blue *sbernia* with a golden lining.

Most scholars have dated the painting about 1483, just after Leonardo's arrival in Milan. This view is based upon the correspondence between Cecilia Gallerani, a lady of the Sforza court, and Isabella d'Este. In a letter of 1497, Cecilia wrote that she was quite young at the time when Leonardo painted her, and that she was

14) Leonardo da Vinci, *Lady with an Ermine*, Czartoryski Collection, Cracow.

15) Leonardo da Vinci, *La Belle Ferronnière*, 1490–95, detail, Louvre, Paris.

no longer like the portrait. Nevertheless, it cannot be proved that she is in fact the subject of the *Lady with an Ermine*. We do not know any Milanese portrait of around 1483 showing Spanish dress; almost all those portraits in which the fashion appears were painted about 1490 and in the next decade, at the time of the great matrimonial connections of Milan, Ferrara, and Naples. It would therefore seem correct to date the *Lady with an Ermine* about 1490.

Leonardo's Knots

The sitter's gown in the *Lady with an Ermine* is decorated with specific ornaments known as "Leonardo's knots" (*nodi di Leonardo*). No scholar has paid any attention to them, possibly because they are located in the dark portions of the picture and are partly deformed by repainting.

Three different types of ornaments may be discerned: First, double loops in figure-of-eight form repeated in an endless system (on the edge of the décolletage and on the sleeves); second, endless knots, slightly deformed, repeated in square fields (on the right side of the bodice, as well as at the top of the right sleeve); and third, knots as above with the addition of quatrefoil loops (on the left sleeve under the layer of red paint, visible only when lighted from a certain angle).

A comparative basis for the problem is offered by the knots Leonardo drew in his manuscripts, in particular in the *Codice Atlantico*; the emblematic etchings founded on the knots and interlacing motifs with the inscription *Leonardi Vinci Academia*, which are attributed to Leonardo, and woodcut copies of them made by Albrecht Dürer; the mural decoration of the Sala delle Asse in the Castello Sforzesco in Milan; and finally, by the analogous motifs of knots and loops in the costume decorations of certain other paintings by Leonardo.

There is also literary evidence. Vasari noted Leonardo's passion for knot designs; it is also known that he himself took such designs from Florence to Milan. Scholars were intrigued by these knots very early on, the French positivists J. D. Passavant and G. d'Adda explaining them as patterns for costume embroidery. More recently the interpretation was greatly broadened, as some symbolic intricacies were presumed. Ludwig Goldscheider put forward the suggestion that the emblematic engravings represented tickets for scientific debates organized by Leonardo, and read in the knots a cryptographic signature of the painter, based on a pun from *vincire* (to lace, to knot) and Vinci. Ananda K. Coomaraswamy interpreted the emblems as an old labyrinth subject or even a universal form denoting the cosmos. Mircea Eliade explained the knots as an ancient magic sign and an attribute of such Indo-European gods as Varuna, Ahriman, and Odin. Marcel Brion, in summing up the opinions of his predecessors, also stressed the symbolic values of Leonardo's knots.

These investigations were largely devoid of analysis of the forms Leonardo's knots take. Here the knots may be divided into several groups. Some of them simply repeat mainly Moorish and Turkish patterns, others are free variations on Oriental motifs, while still others are the artist's invention based on the European ornamental tradition.

Particularly important is the endless knot applied both in the emblematic compositions and in the gown decoration of the *Lady with an Ermine*. Deriving from the Far East, it belongs, as the sign of longevity, to the set of Eight Lucky Symbols of Buddhism. This sign was extremely popular and spread from one country to another, appearing on vessels, textiles, rugs, jewels, coins, and arms from at least the twelfth century. It came to Italy as early as the fourteenth century and is found, for instance, in Luccan textiles, but was much more in fashion by the second half of the fifteenth century, especially in Venice. Leonardo's drawings of the endless knot have survived in several places in the *Codice Atlantico*.

Thus we find in the costume and headdress of the *Lady with an Ermine* specific motifs of Oriental derivation: the Moorish-inspired Spanish style and the ancient, enigmatic knots.

MARIA RZEPIŃSKA

Some Questions About the Model for the *Lady with an Ermine*

Leonardo da Vinci's *Lady with an Ermine* holds an exceptional place among the portraits of the late Quattrocento. The painting is connected stylistically with the artist's Florentine period in terms of its small size, the proportion of the figure to the background, and the sharp delicacy of forms. Yet at the same time it is a pioneering work with regard to the placement of the figure in space and the creation of the psychological atmosphere.

The ermine, full of grace and painted with such mastery that it alone could provide sufficient proof of Leonardo's authorship, greatly contributes to this atmosphere. The role of the animal and its correct name have been the subject of much discussion. In the Italian literature the animal is variously identified as a *faina, martora, ermellino,* or *furetto.* But as its coat is distinctly white, despite the yellowing and darkening of the painted surface, there is no doubt that it is an ermine, although the head is a trifle broad. The names ermine and weasel are not in fact contradictory. The ermine is a species of weasel in its winter coat. Nevertheless, the historians contrasted the meanings of the words *faina* and *ermellino* because the weasel was considered the symbol of debauchery and the ermine that of chastity.

Marian Sokołowski (1892) and Jerzy Mycielski (1893) connected this symbolism with the Cracow painting, recalling that the ermine was the emblem of Anne de Bretagne, the wife of Louis XII, and was also thought to be a device of Ludovico Sforza. W. von Seidlitz (1906) held the view that the painting is not a portrait at all but rather an allegory of *castitas.* Later it was realized that the Greek word *galē,* meaning ermine, is part of the name Gallerani.

Since we accept the authorship of Leonardo, even with the participation of a pupil, it is more than probable that the picture represents Cecilia Gallerani, Ludovico's mistress, one of the most enchanting women at the court of Milan. This love affair began when she was about sixteen years old. After the birth of their first child in 1487, Ludovico gave Cecilia the property of Saronno. The second son, born in 1491, received a ducal title. After his marriage to Beatrice d'Este, Ludovico had to part with Cecilia and so he married her to Count Ludovico Carminati-Bergamini. The couple took up residence in the palace of Carmagnola (now called Del Verme). Matteo Bandello mentions that Cecilia had a salon where she entertained scholars, musicians, and artists. The critic and poet Ortensio Lando compared her to Isabella d'Este and Vittoria Colonna.

Leonardo probably painted Cecilia when she was sixteen. That she was very young we know from a letter which she wrote to Isabella d'Este in answer to the latter's request to borrow the painting.

The portrait of Cecilia caused a sensation. The court poet Bernardo Bellincioni (?–1492) praised it in a sonnet, and later Giulio Cesare Scaliger (1484–1558) also extolled it; he probably saw it in Cecilia's palace near Cremona, where it remained presumably until her death in 1536.

Nothing was heard of the portrait from the beginning of the sixteenth until the end of the eighteenth century; nowhere is it mentioned. Only C. Amoretti, librarian of the Ambrosiana in Milan, supplied information in a book published in 1804:

Trovo fra le note mss. del De Pagave, che il ritratto della Gallerani, maritata poi al conte Lodovico Bergamino, vedevasi ancora a Milano nel secolo ora scorso presso i marchesi Bonasana, e una bella e antica copia n'abbiamo nella nostra galleria.

In 1900, the Polish art historian Józef Bołoz-Antoniewicz identified the painting in Cracow as the "lost" portrait of Cecilia on the basis of Amoretti's note, Bellincioni's sonnet, and the references by Bandello and Scaliger, as well as on the approximate date of the picture's purchase in Italy by Prince Adam Jerzy Czartoryski. Bołoz-Antoniewicz gave the date of Bellincioni's death, 1492, as the date *ad quem* of the portrait.

It should be stressed that at that time very few scholars considered Leonardo the author of the Cracow painting; at most it was seen as the work of one of his pupils.

Bołoz-Antoniewicz was the first scholar not only to identify the model but also to assert without hesitation the authorship of Leonardo. Unfortunately, as his study was published only in Polish and summarized in a publication with a very limited circulation, it did not meet with a wide response. Some Italian and German scholars knew it but only G. Carotti and W. Suida at once supported Bołoz-Antoniewicz's views.

When the painting was taken to Dresden for the duration of the First World War, it became more accessible for scholarly examination. In 1916, E. Moeller published an extensive paper acknowledging the authorship of Leonardo and the identity of the model as Cecilia. The opinion of this renowned art historian did have an impact. Nevertheless, numerous scholars rejected the attribution to Leonardo, naming instead Boltraffio, Ambrogio da Predis, or Bernardino dei Conti as possible authors, even as late as 1942. But many scholars who had previously doubted Leonardo's authorship, including A. Venturi and Bernard Berenson, changed their minds.

On the quatercentenary of Leonardo's death a long article by Henryk Ochenkowski, curator of the Czartoryski Gallery, was published in both Italian and English, with an exhaustive bibliography. This paper became far better known than the breakthrough study by Bołoz-Antoniewicz, to which the author added new arguments, taken from the writings of Leonardo, on the subject of Ludovico's emblem. Kenneth Clark in his monograph of 1939 included the Cracow painting among the master's works.

The *Lady with an Ermine* was the focal point of an exhibition of Italian art held at the Czartoryski Gallery in 1961. Soon afterwards, Zdzisław Żygulski published an extensive paper in which he analyzed the model's costume in detail. He showed that the garments and coiffure of Cecilia conform to a fashionable style borrowed from Spain. The cape draped over her left shoulder is the Spanish *sbernia*, while the hairstyle was called *el tranzado*. The lady's necklace is made of black amber, popular at the time and sometimes seen in portraits. Żygulski recalled the work on costumes by Schiapparelli, who attributed the introduction of the fashion *alla spagnuola* at the court of Milan to Isabella of Aragon. Because Spanish dress does not appear in any other portraits from Milan before about 1490, Żygulski shifted the date of the *Lady with an Ermine* from 1483–85 to *c.* 1490, and this date is now in the catalogue of the Czartoryski Collection. However, the earlier date seems more probable in view of Cecilia's extreme youth and is generally accepted.

The issue appears somewhat differently in the light of Rosita L. Pisetzky's two-volume *Storia del costume in Italia* (Milan, 1964). The author claims that this type of hairstyle and headdress was especially preferred in fifteenth-

16) Leonardo da Vinci, *Mona Lisa*, 1503–05, Louvre, Paris.

Pisetzky, such a headdress was mainly worn by unmarried girls until Beatrice d'Este introduced it for married women as well.

The author also says that the model in Leonardo's *Lady with an Ermine* is wearing, in addition to the fillet and veil, a black silk hair-net (*crea* or *santuzio*), closely wrapped around the head and bound under the chin. So it is not a later repainting, especially as a similar hair-net can be seen on the head of another model in an anonymous painting of *c.* 1490. The *lenza* was also called *ferronnière*.

As for the dating of Cecilia's portrait, a Leonardo expert from the University of California, Carlo Pedretti, believes it might have something to do with the decoration of Ludovico Sforza by the king of Naples with the Order of the Ermine in 1488. Pedretti points out that Leonardo's drawing of the allegory of the ermine is in the same style as his anatomical studies of *c.* 1489.

To return to Żygulski, he also drew attention to the similarities between the embroidery motifs on the gown and the well-known *nodi vinciani*. These braid and knot designs, which are very likely of Oriental origin, occur in Leonardo's notebooks nearly throughout his life, the earliest ones dating from about 1480. Similar motifs appear on the gown of the model in *The Madonna of the Rocks* and also on some of the garments worn in female portraits painted by members of Leonardo's circle.

These portraits are variants of the *Beatrice d'Este* type (Pinacoteca Ambrosiana, Milan) and *La Belle Ferronnière* (Louvre, Paris) [Fig. 15]. Considering the great quantity of copies and variants which were also inspired by the *Mona Lisa* [Fig. 16], it seems strange that the famous portrait which Isabella d'Este was so anxious to see did not find any imitators. We would be justified, however, in supposing that paintings modelled on Cecilia's portrait did exist. They were still to be found in Milan in Amoretti's lifetime, in the early nineteenth century. One of them represented St. Cecilia holding a zither. The other repeated Leonardo's portrait of Cecilia Gallerani but showed her as an older woman. Amoretti writes about it:

Questa rinomata donna qui è dipinta come nel primo ritratto fattole dal Leonardo medesimo nei tempi della fiorente sua giovinezza; ma invece della cetra, essa sembra tenere colla mano una piega della veste.

century Italy. The plaited queue of hair was called *coazzone* and the fillet binding it *trinzale*. A picture by Domenico Ghirlandajo is reproduced in volume II showing two kneeling donors, Isabella Aldobrandini and Violanta Malatesta, who have sleek hairstyles with tightly bound *coazzone*, thin fillets (*lenza*) across the forehead, transparent veils, square necklines on the bodice, and separately attached laced sleeves. According to

One may assume that the pose was very similar, only instead of an ermine the model was holding a zither in the first picture and a fold of her gown in the second.

Although the attribution of the Cracow portrait has now been accepted almost unanimously by scholars, doubts as to the identity of the model are being expressed. The trouble is that in Bellincioni's sonnet praising the portrait there is not a word about the ermine.

In this writer's view, however, that fact does not prove anything. In Renaissance records of works of art we never find such exactitude as would now be required. Vasari's description of the *Mona Lisa* gives a detailed account of the figure's complexion, the pores of her skin, and the hair of her eyebrows, yet never mentions the strange landscape in the background or even the famous hands. We know that Vasari could not have seen the painting himself as it was in France, but other examples of faulty or incomplete descriptions might be cited, even in cases where Vasari must have seen the originals—and he was a painter and biographer. What then, can one expect of poetry, with its imposed model whereby above all the idea of "matching" or "surpassing" nature prevailed? The scheme is known from numerous epigrams, epitaphs, and commemorative poems. Thus it is not surprising that we find it in Bellincioni's sonnet. The poet was more concerned with the perfection of the poem than with the faithfulness of the description and therefore kept to the commonly accepted conventions.

The only fragment of Bellincioni's sonnet which seems to have a direct connection with the Cracow painting are the words "par che ascolti, e non favella." Indeed, the model, with youthful gaiety, seems to be listening attentively to something. Her movement and her pose are permeated with the *prontitudine* mentioned so often in Leonardo's writings. W. N. Lazarev rightly recalled that Leonardo was very fond of cyphered emblems, including the ermine in the portrait of Cecilia Gallerani and the juniper in the background and on the back of the *Portrait of Ginevra de' Benci* (Ginevra, *genaprio*) [Fig. 8].

That none of the old sources mentions Leonardo's painting of a lady with an ermine is mysterious, as is the fact that the portrait surfaced only after 1800. If we knew more of the circumstances surrounding Prince Czartoryski's purchase of the painting, such information might help dispel the doubts. Unfortunately, nothing on the subject has been found in the Czartoryski archives, part of which were irrevocably destroyed. One should bear in mind, however, that even the identification of the model for the *Mona Lisa* has been questioned.

KAROL ESTREICHER

Some Remarks on the X-Rays of the *Lady with an Ermine*

All researchers agree that the *Lady with an Ermine* by Leonardo da Vinci dates from the late fifteenth century, and more likely from the 1480s than after 1490. The evidence lies in both the costume and the silhouette: the somewhat dryly treated figure, the very plastic, almost sculptural hand, and finally the detailed, miniature-like breaking of the folds at the sleeve slits. At the very end of the century such features would not have appeared in the work of either Leonardo or his pupils.

The girl's right hand holding the ermine is painted with immense maturity and a wonderfully light brush. It is not free from repainting but this whole area of the portrait shows excellence of brush. The hand with its long thin fingers is handled with great plasticity; one can sense the bones through the transparent skin.

The painting of the ermine is on the same high level. Its veracity and expressiveness make it one of the finest details in the portrait.

Despite repainting in places, the face and breast are done with a mastery that raises the picture far above ordinary paintings and copies.

All the more striking, therefore, are certain peculiar flaws: the repainting in the hair and the dress, the hairband across the forehead, the beads, and worst of all, the fact that the glossy dark background brutally overlaps the figure, to the detriment of the plasticity of its outline. Thus, a feature so characteristic of Leonardo—the smooth outline of an internally animated figure—is unpleasantly underlined, something which could never have come from the master's hand. Also jarring is the way the girl's left hand vanishes into shadow, whereby the fingers are cut off. This hand does not seem to be on the same artistic level as the right one.

Can these weak points be attributed to repainting? Perhaps not all of them. The flat black background is the result of an improper restoration probably carried out in the eighteenth century, when the inscription in the upper left corner of the painting was added. However, some of the problems seem to have been present almost from the very beginning.

The portrait was not damaged during World War II. Wrapped in a blanket and tightly packed in a box, it safely withstood its repeated transfers. Only the upper left corner, which was previously damaged, became detached. When the painting arrived in Munich in 1945, it required only minor restoration.

Its storage in Munich among countless other artworks pillaged by the Nazis offered an opportunity for comparison with the most magnificent Renaissance paintings. The flaws in the portrait as well as its outstanding qualities could be more easily distinguished.

The painting was X-rayed at the Dörner Institute in Munich. Thus it is possible to see the deepest parts of the painting on the border between the ground and the walnut panel—the initial stage when the artist was concentrating on capturing the model's likeness. As is usual at the beginning of a portrait, different parts of the painting were not evenly handled. The artist gave his attention primarily to the outline of the figure, its position, the basic lighting, the major elements such as the hands and body, and to the likeness, so difficult to master if not caught at the outset.

The face, the hand, and the shoulders are clear in the X-ray photograph. A full analysis allows us to distinguish between what is seen on the painted surface and its origins or design.

In the X-ray, the face is softer, subtler, and fuller. The differences are barely perceptible, but they exist. The main reason for the fuller oval of the face is that the hair is not shown tied under the chin, and the cheekbones are very strongly marked. The original nose and eyes are also different. The forehead is more salient and the nose seems to be a little shorter and fuller, slightly retroussé, and roundish as if modelled. In the finished painting the nose stands out sharply against the left cheek and does not appear in the X-ray. Also, in the X-ray the mouth seems more distorted; this is the first attempt at this strange foreshortening of the lips in the grimace which gives the sitter her remarkable expression—the first attempt at animating the face with a smile.

The right hand is in the same place as on the surface of the painting, but at this first stage it was treated more sketchily than the face. It is basically the same beautiful hand with long sculpted fingers. The X-ray scarcely shows traces of the outline of the ermine's head, suggesting it was not painted at this stage.

17) Leonardo da Vinci, *Study of Female Hands*, Royal Library, Windsor Castle.

There is neither an outline of the left hand nor any decoration or folds in the costume. There are no beads; they may have been added later. The hair is barely indicated.

Apart from the face, the main differences concern that border between the figure and the background. What is so jarring in the portrait disappears completely in the X-ray: the figure is softly and smoothly drawn out from the background, it has some space behind it, it is not a pasted-over cutout. The transition from the background to the figure is gradual, enhancing the plasticity. The play of light and shade (Vasari claimed Leonardo invented it) was intended to be much livelier.

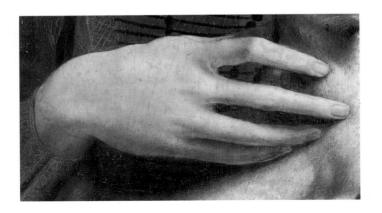

18) Leonardo da Vinci, *Lady with an Ermine*, detail.

19) Leonardo da Vinci, *Mona Lisa*, detail.

There was no background in the original stage. The face, younger and more girlish than that which we see in the portrait, was painted straight onto the walnut panel. The artist very likely worked on the rest without the model.

The face is related to Leonardo's angel in Andrea del Verrocchio's *Baptism of Christ* (Uffizi Gallery, Florence). The same expression also appears on an angel's face in *The Virgin of the Rocks* (Louvre, Paris)—the nose is well shaped and roundish, the lips are tightly drawn, and the cheekbones are emphasized by the use of shadow.

T. Gerevich noticed that the hands in sketch 210 at Windsor Castle are stylistically related to the hands in the portrait. This is confirmed in the X-ray photograph. Leonardo sketched the right hand in the same manner in which he then finished it. The long, bent, bony fingers are different from the hands in the *Mona Lisa* [Fig. 19]. In the *Lady with an Ermine*, Leonardo seems to have followed a pattern of hands treated sculpturally with bony fingers. The type was characteristic for Verrocchio, as in his *Lady with Primroses* or the terra-cotta relief of the Madonna and Child (Bargello, Florence).

Does the hand holding the ermine simply reflect the real model and not any artistic scheme received in the school of sculpture? There is obviously no easy answer to this question. It should be noted that a) the similarities to Verrocchio's works appear to be too strong to be considered casual, and for someone as young as Leonardo was at the time, they are very plausible and justifiable; and b) the individualization of the hands that can be seen in such works by Leonardo as the *Mona Lisa*, only appeared in Italian painting towards the end of the fifteenth century, probably under Netherlandish influence.

To sum up, the X-ray of the *Lady with an Ermine* reveals the portrait's close links with Florentine painting, more specifically with Leonardo's Florentine period, which demonstrates that the artist painted it shortly after his arrival in Milan.

34

RUDOLF KOZŁOWSKI

An Examination of *Lady with an Ermine*

To determine the authenticity of Leonardo da Vinci's *Lady with an Ermine*, this author conducted an examination of the painting in February 1952. A sample of the undercoat was taken from the very edge of the painting and examined under microscope. The picture was studied under ultraviolet rays, a binocular magnifying glass, and a microscope.

The microchemically examined sample of ground, in contrast to the gesso or, rarely, calcite with animal glue used in Italy at the time, appeared to be Kremnitz white bound with oil or egg-yolk tempera. The method of grounding the walnut panel was that the ground was only pressed into the irregularities and pores of the wood. This distinguishes the *Lady with an Ermine* from contemporary Italian works since the gesso ground of most medieval and Renaissance paintings produces an always distinctive white layer of varying thickness. The preparation of the ground in Leonardo's portrait is clearly visible from earlier X-ray photographs.

The introduction of Kremnitz white with an oil binder as a ground and breaking with the tradition of using a gesso and glue layer primer, was a revolutionary invention, anticipating the later use of such materials on wood.

The ground in the portrait remarkably exemplifies the experimental methods of the author of *The Last Supper*. This kind of ground probably could not have been used by Leonardo's pupils Giovanni Antonio Boltraffio or Ambrogio da Predis, since they copied the more developed Renaissance style of the later Leonardo with a characteristic glazing ground borrowed from Flemish painting.

Leonardo maintained the grounds of his later paintings in the browns he favored, and the glazing ground technique required a layer of white ground made of gesso or chalk bound with animal glue.

The walnut panel of the portrait, filled rather than grounded with Kremnitz white, could not have been the ground for the later technique using glazing grounds. This kind of ground points to Leonardo's early Florentine or Milanese period. According to Kiplik, Leonardo used tempera in that period. This writer's examination of the portrait reconfirmed the accepted assertions about the features of Leonardo's Florentine style, which retained influences from Verrocchio's workshop.

In the lower left corner of the painting, I noticed a small, previously unknown mark which could be read as a signature consisting of two letters painted with a brush. This is a letter "L" written upside down with the left hand and connecting with the letter "V". Microscopic examination of the signature revealed cracking of paint that is slightly weaker than in the surrounding area, excluding, however, the recent origin of the signature. Its dark greenish grey color is similar to the tone of fillings made on the brighter and greener ribbons decorating the sleeves of the sitter's costume. Under ultraviolet examination, the signature shows the same lack of luminescence as the ribbon fillings, which would suggest that these parts were not painted at the same time as the rest of the picture.

Studying a collection of Leonardo's handwriting samples, I found similarities with the signature in the portrait both in the general character of the handwriting, marked by dominant vertical strokes, and in the decline of the horizontal lines. In all variants of the artist's handwriting and in the portrait signature the same specific rhythm of graphic characters appears. The resemblance between the signature and Leonardo's handwriting is strongest where a cut or rounding of a worn-out pen makes the characters look as if they were written with a brush.

The following questions arise in connection with the signature:

1) Is the signature contemporary with the painting of the portrait?

2) Was it added later by Leonardo himself after the application of varnish, using a different pigment and binder, which was also used to correct the sleeve ribbons?

3) Or was the original signature repainted later by someone who made some color corrections to make it stand out better?

4) Or finally, was the signature added by some unknown painter who completed the ribbons with a few brushstrokes and was evidently familiar with Leonardo's signature? He could only have painted the signature knowing that the author of the portrait was indeed Leonardo.

The examination of the portrait for the effects of restorations produced stronger arguments for Leonardo's authorship. As for the retouches which were thought to have spoiled the composition, basically only the dull black background is the result of repainting. Besides some cor-

rections in places, including the hair, the beads, and black details of the costume, lights were added to the eyes [Fig. 20] and vertical cracks on the arm and on the animal's head and body were shaded.

Except for the retouching of the vertical cracks in original paint, all other retouches (fortunately not numerous) were incompetent corrections to make up for the loss of the original paint which was destroyed as a result of careless cleaning during a previous restoration. The damaged parts were primarily the most delicate finishing layers and glazes in shades. A retouch laid on a damaged lower part of the nose done schematically without sensitivity for Leonardo's form, is one of the factors contributing to some conventionality in the plastic aspect of the head. From tiny remains of brown finishing glazes found on the left cheek, it can be assumed that the face and arm were more strongly modelled and thereby merged into the background instead of standing out as they do now. The repainted background emphasizes all the more the lack of massiveness where the complexion meets the black background paint.

The most delicate surface glazes must have been painted in oil with increased additions of resin, causing them to deteriorate faster. However, the face and breast were finished in the basic paint layer, so the loss of subtle glazes that once deepened and refined the colors is not as disturbing.

Microphotographs of the figure's silhouette against the background show differences in the black pigment. Near her right shoulder the background is slightly cracked, dull, and flat, the result of the last repainting, whereas near the left shoulder, neck, blue sleeve, and the top part of the hair, the black color is deeper and the cracks are wholly consistent with the above-mentioned parts of the painting. The pattern of cracks suggests that the black paint is not original, but rather part of either an earlier, first repainting of the background or outlining of the figure, because on this occasion the cheek, neck, and shoulder were slightly cut and the original shade between the blue gown and the shoulder was modified by a black outline. The background was most likely maintained in dark brown and greenish tones which expressed the spatiality of the interior. This conclusion is confirmed by earlier X-ray photographs which do not register light, X-ray absorbent pigments, with the exception of the Kremnitz white ground pressed into irregularities of the board and the pores of the wood grains.

Every restorer knows how easily this kind of background can be damaged during careless restoration. Therefore, it is clear that the smearing with the black oily substance was intended to cover the destruction of the genuine background.

If we imagine that the background was not flat but rather expressed the dark space of a room, and if we add that the portrait was more strongly modelled and thus organically connected with the dark background of the room, then we can easily imagine that the face, breast, and arms and the rest of the lit and bright parts of the painting create one harmonious unit. The best preserved parts, such as the ermine and the right hand, testify to the painter's mastery.

Dark parts of the painting were also retouched rather than repainted. The left hand, concealed in deep shadow and unfinished, could not contain more details. From the assumption of composition it can be seen that it must have been treated more synthetically. This hand, well connected with the composition, shows some unjustified lighter and darker patches, which can only be attributed to wrong-headed restoration attempts.

On the left sleeve can be seen, in the painting's oblique lighting, a vivid ornament of the embroidered dress piercing the layer of dark orange paint with which the dress eventually was finished. From the nature of cracks in the paint evidently laid on an incompletely dried bottom layer, it can be assumed that most probably Leonardo repainted the dress and abandoned the idea of embroidery on the sleeves in favor of emphasizing the rhythms of an ornament formed by bows fastening the sleeve slits.

The high artistic value of the painting suffers not only from the repainting of the background and the retouching, but even more from unskillful restorations which caused the loss of the subtle finishing brushstrokes of the greatest master of the Italian Renaissance.

KAZIMIERZ KWIATKOWSKI

Scientific Analysis of the *Lady with an Ermine*

Physical Examination: X-Ray Photographs

X-ray photographs of the *Lady with an Ermine* show a weak distinctness of the outlines, which are gentle and dissolving. They also show the absence of contrasts in some parts of the paint.

The structure of a painted surface has a consistent character. Densities are smooth and soft. Dynamic *impastos* were not used. The grain is clearly visible throughout the painted surface, showing enough of the wood structure to allow an identification of the wood as walnut panel. However, the grain is invisible within one centimeter of the edges of the painting.

The distinctness of the grain probably stems from the fact that the material used for the ground strongly absorbs X-rays. By filling the porous and fibrous surface of the walnut panel, this material reinforced the contrasts on the whole surface of the painting and underlined the structure of the wood. As there is no ground on the edge, the grains are invisible in that area. This observation leads to the conclusions that the painting must have been framed when painted and that it has preserved its original dimensions.

The experts determined that the panel was part of a trunk whose center should be 7 to 8 centimeters to the left of the painting's axis, which means that from this trunk, boards a few centimeters wider could also have been cut.

Cracks occur as quite regular vertical, horizontal, and diagonal lines. The first two depend to some degree on wood fibers and their movement, and therefore maintain their general direction, whereas diagonal lines go through the whole face, the neck, and hair, and partly through the background, producing a series of fairly parallel lines resembling in their rhythmic intervals hatching.

In the upper left corner and in the background near the head, some repairs can be seen (lead fillings). Minor losses in the background are probably the result of mechanical damages.

X-ray photographs did not register the hair reaching down around the chin. According to Renaissance methods of painting, the hair, eyebrows, and hair-band were probably painted on an already formed shape, taking advantage of the qualities of glazes and half-glazes. In our case, the complexion was painted with a mixture of flesh tones lightened with Kremnitz white and Neapolitan yellow, which absorb X-rays most highly, and this was registered in the X-ray photograph. The hair, especially near the chin, and the beads were painted in dark organic pigments, which do not absorb X-rays as much as heavy metal compounds and therefore did not show up. Consequently, it seems unlikely that these parts of the painting were painted later.

The X-rays show no sign of significant changes in the conception of the painting apart from slight deviations resulting from the search for an adequate plastic expression.

Ultraviolet Examination

Ultraviolet examination shows many small retouches, put on a thick layer of phosphorescent varnish, as well as many corrections to the ribbons, beads, hair, and hair-band. The retouches come from several restorations carried out at quite distant times, but their precise dating is difficult because of the absence of archival records. Very likely the background was repainted several times during consecutive restorations and the repainting was done in parts. This is indicated by the type of pigments and damages in the background, which is densely and broadly covered with dark paint. The dark background partly covered up the blue garment and the bare part of the shoulder to the detriment of its silhouette. It is shown by flaking of repaintings uncovering the flesh tints of the complexion and robes under the background. The inscription also must have been written during one of the restorations. Spelling mistakes in "La Bele Feroniere. Leonard D'Awinci," and the introduction of the letter "W," may indicate a Polish origin. The style of the letters is from the end of the eighteenth or beginning of the nineteenth century.

There is much less varnish on the surface of the background, as can be clearly seen in the photograph—there is no luminescence. The right arm and hair on the neck are covered with a much thicker layer of varnish, possibly covering the original varnish. It could be assumed that a similar layer is present under the repaintings of the background. Damages in the background near the head, which measure about two millimeters in diameter and are of mechanical origin, are covered with black paint of the same quality as the one in the background of the painting and retouches (on the X-ray the losses were registered as deep ones). On very close examination something like an architectural fragment can be detected on the right side of the background. Its outline is vanishing and it looks like a silhouette of an entrance or a broadly sketched window.

In the original composition there were apparently attempts to introduce into the painting architectural fragments such as an interior, a window, or an entrance. They could have been abandoned by the author in subsequent stages of the work and covered with paint in order to simplify and unite the composition with a heightened focus on the figure. A window need not be significant, as it is characteristic for Leonardo and his circle. The *Madonna Benois* and the *Madonna Litta* (Hermitage, St. Petersburg), as well as many pencil sketches, prove that the sketched architectural fragments were probably done in asphalt paint, which Leonardo is known to have used.

Infrared Examinations

Infrared examination shows the individual lines of the original drawing of the hairstyle, eyebrows, and a double outlined iris in the left eye. The sketching is particularly distinctive on the left shoulder of the girl. One can assume that first the outlines of the reddish brown gown were sketched and then the blue cape was added. A soft brush and a paint of liquid consistency were used for the sketch. Strokes around the animal's head and a sketch of a middle part of the girl's breast were made in the same way. They are completely invisible to the naked eye. The infrared examination also discovers vertical, horizontal, and in particular diagonal cracks. The latter are clearly visible on the left cheek and the neck. Cracks on the gown near the right hand are different, probably due to their asphalt origin.

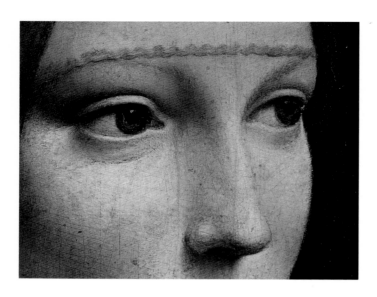

20) Leonardo da Vinci, *Lady with an Ermine*, detail.

Photographs

Photographs show an extremely smooth and thinly spread film of paint on the hands, face, and neck, obtained by applying one layer of paint after another, and by glazes and half-glazes. The effect is enamel-like transparency in the shadows and flesh-colored materiality in the illuminated parts of the skin.

The network of cracks appears here almost analogically to the X-ray photographs, maintaining the same direction and repeated rhythm of vertical, horizontal, and diagonal lines. The resemblance is particularly striking in the case of diagonal cracks. On the painted surface they are clearer and more distinctive. This leads to the hypothesis that the diagonal cracks may be the equivalent of the original sketch graded with lines since they are regular and underline the shape of the shaded part of the face. The diagonal cracks also appear, though fewer in number, in the hair and in the lit areas. A crack on the outline of the tip of the nose [Fig. 20] does not seem to be accidental. It takes a different direction

from that of the diagonal cracks, and is rather streamlined. This can also be observed in Leonardo's other works, where similar cracks appear near the end of a nose, albeit in a somewhat different way. Nevertheless, in areas where a sketch was prepared longer and more carefully, cracks occur more easily and go against the direction of the wood.

The clearly visible diagonal cracks on the face are similar in direction to those present in *La Belle Ferronnière* (Louvre, Paris) [Fig. 15]. They could have developed as a result of the weaker adhesion of paint in the places of the sketch, graded with a pencil or a pen. Moreover, the direction of these lines seems to indicate that the author was left-handed, and recall Leonardo's drawings graded in pen or pencil.

The suggestion of a left-handed line concerns also individual hairs on the eyebrows and eyelashes, and traces of brushstrokes in the white of the eye. Brushstrokes are made with either the right or the left hand depending on the direction of the stroke and on the tool used. It would thus be reasonable to assume that Leonardo not only wrote and drew with both his left and his right hand but also painted this way. It is very likely that the eye on the right side was painted with the right hand, and the one on the left with the left hand. This is indicated by the traces of brush touches on the white of the right eye and the clear original outline of the iris of the left eye.

The directions of the brushstrokes, "the character of handwriting," are best shown on the animal's fur. It is modelled with a long, confident line, a thin brush, and silver-yellow covering paint. In terms of technique, it is undoubtedly the most readable part of the painting; elsewhere the smooth surface conceals the technique. This exceptional clarity of almost every single brushstroke enables us to tell where it begins and ends. The end is always sharp and dry as opposed to the start of a stroke, which is thicker and more richly covered with paint. Therefore, after a thorough examination of the brush motion traces, it can be assumed that the fur on the animal's head and body was painted with both left- and right-handed strokes.

In the lower left corner a sign, or monogram, in the form of two interlaced letters can be seen. The sign was found to be on a thicker layer of varnish. In addition, the sign covers the network of cracks in the paint. This leads to the conclusion that it was painted much later when the painting had been varnished several times and the cracks already existed.

Under these circumstances it would be difficult to regard the signature as authentic, especially since Leonardo never signed his paintings.

Conclusion

1) The panel was already framed when the ground was prepared with Kremnitz white and was not cut later.

2) The structure of the paint film over the whole surface is consistent and together with the compositional unity points to the work's single authorship.

3) The chiaroscuro and the composition of the drawing seem to have been adapted for a left hand.

a) Diagonal lines of cracks on the cheek, hair, and torso can be regarded as the equivalents of left-handed lines in the original sketch.
b) The hair on the animal's head and ears was produced with both the left and right hand.
c) The eye and the part of the face on the left side of the portrait were painted with the left hand, while the other part of the face was painted with the right hand.

4) It can be concluded that the author of the painting was both left- and right-handed. Leonardo is known to have used both hands in writing and drawing, and this fact fully confirms his authorship of this work.

CHRONOLOGY

1452	Birth of Leonardo da Vinci in Tuscany.
c. 1482	Leonardo arrives in Milan to work at the court of Duke Ludovico Sforza ("il Moro").
1483–85	Presumed date of Leonardo's *Portrait of a Lady with an Ermine* (thought to be Cecilia Gallerani).
before 1492	Court poet Bernardo Bellincioni (*d.* 1492) composes a sonnet devoted to Leonardo's portrait of Cecilia Gallerani.
April 26, 1498	Isabella d'Este of Mantua writes to Cecilia Gallerani asking to borrow Leonardo's portrait of her for comparison with portraits painted by Giovanni Bellini.
April 29, 1498	In her reply to Isabella d'Este's letter, Cecilia Gallerani agrees to lend her the portrait.
April-May, 1498	Leonardo's portrait of Cecilia Gallerani is sent from Milan to Mantua and back.
1519	Death of Leonardo at Cloux, near Amboise, France.
1536	Death of Cecilia Gallerani.
1536–1800	No information about the portrait; it is rumored to be in the collection of Emperor Rudolf II in Prague at the beginning of the seventeenth century, but no documentation exists of its presence there. The painting is restored shortly before 1800 and the background painted over in black.

21) Maria Cecile Cosway, *Portrait of Princess Isabella Czartoryska*, Czartoryski Collection, Cracow.

22) Andreas Geiger, after Joseph Abel, *Portrait of Prince Adam Jerzy Czartoryski*, Czartoryski Collection, Cracow.

c. 1800   Prince Adam Jerzy Czartoryski purchases the portrait in Italy and donates it to the museum being set up by his mother, Princess Isabella Czartoryska, at her estate in Puławy.

1809–30   The portrait is exhibited in the Green Room of the Gothic House at Puławy along with Raphael's *Portrait of a Young Man* (now lost) and Rembrandt's *Landscape with Tempest* (now known as *Landscape with the Good Samaritan*). Princess Isabella Czartoryska writes the first catalogue notes herself.

1830–31   Polish Uprising of 1830 against Russian rule. The tsar sentences Prince Adam Jerzy Czartoryski, as head of the provisional Polish government, to death in absentia and officially confiscates the property of the Czartoryski family. Princess Isabella Czartoryska, aged 85, saves the art collection, including the portrait by Leonardo, from the advancing Russian army. The portrait is hidden at the Czartoryski residence at Sieniawa and later transferred first to Dresden and then to Paris.

c. 1849–76   The portrait is kept at the Czartoryski residence in Paris, the Hôtel Lambert, but not publicly displayed and there is no information about its presence.

1876   Opening of the Czartoryski Museum in Cracow. The portrait arrives from Paris probably in 1882, together with Raphael's *Portrait of a Young Man*.

1889   Portrait is published for the first time by German art historian P. Müller-Walde.

1900   Polish art historian Józef Bołoz-Antoniewicz first identifies the sitter in the portrait as Cecilia Gallerani. Though challenged from time to time, the identification remains generally accepted.

1914   The portrait is sent to Dresden for safekeeping during the First World War and art historians debate its authorship.

1920   The Gemäldegalerie's efforts to hold on to the portrait fail and it finally leaves Dresden for Cracow.

1939   The Nazis find the portrait in its hiding place at the Czartoryski palace at Sieniawa and send it to Berlin. Initially destined for a planned art museum in Linz, it is given instead to Hans Frank, head of the *Generalgouvernement* in Nazi-occupied Poland.

1941–45   The portrait is sent to Breslau in June 1941, presented at an exhibition at the Wawel Royal Castle in Cracow in March 1943, taken to Sichów Castle in Lower Silesia probably in the summer of 1944, and from there transferred to Hans Frank's villa in Bavaria, where it is found by the Polish-American Committee. The portrait undergoes its first X-ray examination while stored in Munich with numerous other art treasures looted by the Nazis.

1946   Return of the portrait to the Czartoryski Museum in Cracow.

1950–51   The portrait is temporarily housed in Wawel Castle during renovation of the Czartoryski Museum.

1952   The portrait is sent to the National Museum in Warsaw for an exhibition commemorating the 500th anniversary of Leonardo's birth.

1952–54   Kazimierz Kwiatkowski examines the portrait in the laboratory of the National Museum in Warsaw.

1954   Marek Rostworowski publishes a study confirming the date of the portrait as *c.* 1483–85.

1955   Despite government attempts to keep the portrait in the capital, Marek Rostworowski succeeds in bringing it back to Cracow.

1969   Zdzisław Żygulski, Jr., proposes a later date of *c.* 1490 for the portrait on the basis of the sitter's costume.

1972   The painting is presented at an exhibition of European portraiture in the Pushkin Museum in Moscow.

23) Willibald Richter, *View of the Gothic House*, Czartoryski Collection, Cracow.

24) The Czartoryski Museum, Cracow.

1974   The portrait is exhibited at the National Museum in Warsaw on the occasion of the 30th anniversary of the formation of the People's Republic of Poland.

1977   Maria Rzepińska argues for the portrait's original *c.* 1483–85 dating.

1984   The portrait is newly displayed in a separate room in the Picture Gallery of the Czartoryski Museum.

October 1991-January 1992   The portrait is included in the exhibition "Circa 1492. Artists in the Age of Exploration," held at the National Gallery of Art in Washington, in connection with the 500th anniversary of the discovery of America.

SELECTED BIBLIOGRAPHY

—Józef Bołoz-Antoniewicz, "Portret Cecylii Gallerani przez Leonarda da Vinci w Muzeum Książąt Czartoryskich w Krakowie," *Pamiętnik III Zjazdu Historyków Polskich w Krakowie*, Cracow, 1900, pp. 1–9.

—Józef Bołoz-Antoniewicz, *Leonardo da Vinci. W czterechsetletnią rocznicę jego śmierci*, Lwów, 1919.

—Kenneth Clark, *Leonardo da Vinci*, Cambridge, 1939.

—Karol Estreicher, "Portret *Damy z łasicą* Leonarda da Vinci. Uwagi w związku z prześwietleniem obrazu," *Biuletyn Historii Sztuki* XIV (1952), pp. 3–13.

—Rudolf Kozłowski, "Leonarda da Vinci portret damy z gronostajem," *Rozprawy i sprawozdania Muzeum Narodowego w Krakowie* II (1954), Cracow, pp. 39–42.

—Kazimierz Kwiatkowski, *"La Dame à l'hermine" de Leonardo da Vinci. Étude technologique*, Wrocław, 1955.

—Kazimierz Kwiatkowski, "Portret damy z gronostajem Leonarda da Vinci w świetle badań technologicznych," *Rocznik Muzeum Narodowego w Warszawie* II (1957), Warsaw, pp. 531–42.

—E. Moeller, "Leonardos Bildnis der Cecillia Gallerani in der Gallerie des Fürsten Czartoryski in Krakau," *Monatshefte für Kunstwissenschaft* IX (1916), pp. 313–26.

—P. Müller-Walde, "Beiträge zur Kenntnis des Leonardo," *Jahrbuch der Königlichen Preussischen Kunstsammlungen* XX (1899).

—Jerzy Mycielski, *Galerya obrazów przy Muzeum Ks. Czartoryskich w Krakowie*, Cracow, 1893.

—P. Müller-Walde, *Leonardo da Vinci*, Munich, 1889.

—Henryk Ochenkowski, "*La Donna coll'Ermellino* é una composizione di Leonardo da Vinci," *Raccolta Vinciana* X (1919), pp. 65–105.

—Henryk Ochenkowski, *The Quatercentenary of Leonardo da Vinci*, XXXIV, 1916, pp. 186–93.

—Marek Rostworowski, "Leonarda da Vinci portret *Damy z gronostajem*," *Rozprawy i sprawozdania Muzeum Narodowego w Krakowie* II (1954), Cracow, pp. 7–41.

—Maria Rzepińska, *Die "Dame mit dem Hermelin," aus dem Czartoryski-Museum*, Cracow, 1990

—Marian Sokołowski, *Muzeum Czartoryskich w Krakowie*, Lwów, 1892.

—Zdzisław Żygulski, Jr., "Ze studiów nad *Damą z gronostajem*, Styl ubioru i węzły Leonarda," *Biuletyn Historii Sztuki* XXXI, no. 1 (1969), pp. 3–40.

CONTENTS

PREFACE   5
  JÓZEF GRABSKI

INTRODUCTION   6
  MAREK ROSTWOROWSKI

SELECTED SOURCES   8

LEONARDO THE EXPLORER   14
  JANUSZ WAŁEK

LEONARDO DA VINCI'S *LADY WITH AN ERMINE*   19
  MAREK ROSTWOROWSKI

COSTUME STYLE AND LEONARDO'S KNOTS IN THE *LADY WITH AN ERMINE*   24
  ZDZISŁAW ŻYGULSKI, JR.

SOME QUESTIONS ABOUT THE MODEL FOR THE *LADY WITH AN ERMINE*   28
  MARIA RZEPIŃSKA

SOME REMARKS ON THE X-RAYS OF THE *LADY WITH AND ERMINE*   32
  KAROL ESTREICHER

AN EXAMINATION OF *LADY WITH AN ERMINE*   35
  RUDOLF KOZŁOWSKI

SCIENTIFIC ANALYSIS OF THE *LADY WITH AN ERMINE*   38
  KAZIMIERZ KWIATKOWSKI

CHRONOLOGY   42

SELECTED BIBLIOGRAPHY   46